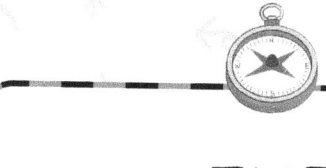

THE
KINDNESS
QUEST

PRAISE FOR THE KINDNESS QUEST

PUPILS' FEEDBACK

EFFIE - YEAR 4

I have learned lots doing **THE KINDNESS QUEST**. I know that a simple smile or a simple hello go a long way in making someone's day.

FINLAY - YEAR 4

When I give my close family or friends a hug or I tell them that I love them, it makes me feel warm inside and it makes my heart full when I see their smile. That's **THE KINDNESS QUEST**.

DINA - YEAR 4

I have loved following **THE KINDNESS QUEST**. Every day I love to fill my happy tank because it helps me to live a happy life just because of one simple act of kindness. It makes me value myself.

ANDRE - YEAR 4

THE KINDNESS QUEST teaches us to be kind, it helps your happiness. It helps maintain your wellbeing and keeps your thoughts in a happy place.

NEVEAH - YEAR 4

THE KINDNESS QUEST teaches us that kindness matters, because if it starts with me it could come back to me when I need it.

LUCIUS - YEAR 4

I really liked doing **THE KINDNESS QUEST**. If you're showing yourself kindness, you can show others the same kindness, making the whole world a better place.

BROOKE - YEAR 4

Doing **THE KINDNESS QUEST** has helped me be a better person. Instead of getting annoyed with people, I walk away which has helped me feel less stressed and means other people want to play with me more. It makes me happier.

BLOOMSBURY EDUCATION
Bloomsbury Publishing Plc
50 Bedford Square, London WC1B 3DP, UK
Bloomsbury Publishing Ireland Limited
29 Earlsfort Terrace, Dublin 2, D02 AY28, Ireland

BLOOMSBURY, BLOOMSBURY EDUCATION and the Diana logo
are trademarks of Bloomsbury Publishing Plc

First published in Great Britain 2025 by Bloomsbury Publishing Plc
This edition published in Great Britain 2025 by Bloomsbury Publishing Plc

A catalogue record for this book is available from the British Library

ISBN: PB: 978-1-8019-9699-0; eBook: 978-1-8019-9720-1;
ePDF: 978-1-8019-9719-5;

2 4 6 8 10 9 7 5 3 1 (paperback)

Text design by Jeni Child

Printed and bound in the UK by CPI Group Ltd, CR0 4YY

To find out more about our authors and books
visit www.bloomsbury.com and sign up for our newsletters
For product safety related questions contact productsafety@bloomsbury.com

THE KINDNESS QUEST

How to be kind to yourself and others

JOHN MAGEE

BLOOMSBURY EDUCATION

LONDON OXFORD NEW YORK NEW DELHI SYDNEY

THE KINDNESS QUEST is dedicated to
my friend, a champion of kindness and outstanding
headteacher from Worsley Mesnes Primary School
in Wigan, Helen Smart. I love and miss you, Helen.
Thank you for being a good friend to me and all the
champions of kindness you created at your school
and the wider community... I will never forget
you and will always hold you dear in my heart.

Special thanks to Headteacher Nichola Hill,
Y5 teacher Rebecca Birchall, and all the pupils
and staff at Meadowbank Primary School.

A special thank you to:

LUCY VALLANCE   ToM PERCIVAL

EMILY EVANS   ADRIAN BETHUNE

CATHY LEAR   ANDREW CoWLEY

BLooMSBURY TEAM   ESTHER SMITH

ARTHUR LUKE   LYNN HoW

MIKE KAWULA   SARAH LAWRENCE

CONTENTS

This book belongs to 9

HOW TO USE THIS BOOK:

An adventurer's guide 14

A teacher's guide 18

A parent/carer's guide 22

Introduction 26

SIX STEPS TO KINDNESS:

Kindness to yourself 32

Kindness at home 47

Kindness at school 59

Kindness to your friends 72

Kindness to your community 83

Kindness to the planet 96

A sparkling conclusion 108

The Kindness Matters community 111

With a heart full of adventure and a thirst for kindness, I embark on this journey to become **RICH IN KINDNESS**! This book is my map, guiding me to become a champion of kindness, spreading joy and happiness along the way.

REMEMBER:

You can personalise this further by adding your creative touch! Draw a picture of yourself embarking on your **KINDNESS QUEST**, or write a short rhyme about the importance of spreading kindness. Make it yours, and have fun!

THIS BOOK BELONGS TO

....

MY QUEST DOESN'T END WITH ME!
HERE'S MY PLEDGE:

1. COMMIT TO KINDNESS:

I commit to diligently doing at least one act of kindness from each step of the book, filling my cup with kindness and happiness.

2. SHARE THE KINDNESS SPARK:

I pledge to share these KINDNESS GEMS with at least .... friends or family members, inspiring them to join my quest.

3. PASS THE TORCH:

I encourage those I share my learnings with to make the same pledge, passing on the torch of kindness and creating a ripple effect of positivity.

SIGNED ....

DATED ....

KINDNESS ADVENTURES

This book welcomes adventurers who yearn to spread kindness, joy, build belonging, meaningful connections, and make the world brighter. If you see yourself in any of these descriptions, this book is waiting to guide you.

THE BUDDING KINDNESS HERO

★ You dream of making a positive difference but need to know where to start.

★ You see kindness as a superpower and want to unlock your potential.

★ You're curious about how small acts can create big ripples of positivity.

THE FRIENDLY EXPLORER:

★ You value friendship and want to nurture and make stronger and more supportive relationships.

★ You believe kindness is the key to building bridges and understanding others.

★ You're eager to learn new ways to show your friends you care.

THE HAPPY-HEARTED ADVENTURER:

★ You're seeking more happiness and inner peace and calm.

★ You understand that kindness is not just about others but also about caring for yourself.

★ You're ready to explore practices that boost your mood and wellbeing.

THE FAMILY FIRST CHAMPION:

★ You want to create a warm and loving home environment for your family.

★ You believe kindness is the glue that strengthens family bonds.

★ You're looking for ways to make everyday moments more meaningful and connected.

THE CHANGEMAKER IN THE MAKING:

★ You see the world's challenges and want to be part of the solution.

★ You believe that kindness can overcome negativity and make a positive impact.

★ You're inspired by others who stand up for what's right and make a difference.

THE POSITIVE PEACEMAKER:

★ You're curious about yourself and want to cultivate self-compassion and kindness.

★ You understand that inner peace is the foundation for outward kindness.

★ You're ready to embark on a journey of self-discovery and growth.

REMEMBER, kindness is a universal language that everyone can speak and understand. So, no matter who you are or what your goals are, **THE KINDNESS QUEST** has something to offer you.

HOW TO
USE THIS BOOK

AN ADVENTURER'S GUIDE

FILL YOUR LIFE
WITH ADVENTURES,
NOT THINGS.
HAVE STORIES TO TELL,
NOT STUFF TO SHOW.

HEY THERE, FELLOW KINDNESS ADVENTURER! This book is your map to becoming **RICH IN KINDNESS** - someone who radiates joy, spreads happiness, and fills the world with sunshine (metaphorically speaking, of course!). But how do you use this map effectively? Worry not, for I'm here to guide you!

Are you a pupil ready to embark on this awesome quest to becoming **RICH IN KINDNESS?** Is that a big yes, I hear you say? Good, here's your plan:

1 Consider a regular goal.
Here's the phrase I use: **'ONE IS BETTER THAN NONE'**. Your goal is to achieve a minimum of one act of kindness in each of the six areas on a regular basis, which will hopefully be easy peasy lemon squeezy.

2 Grab your trusty time machine!
OK, maybe not literally, but set aside a few minutes each day to explore the amazing exercises in this book. Think of it as your daily dose of kindness training!

3 Become a morning superstar!
Start your day with a bang by reading a section from **THE KINDNESS QUEST** and practising its corresponding exercise. Think of it as like brushing your teeth, but for inner kindness!

4 Choose your adventure!
This book is your guide, but you're the captain. Work through the exercises at your own pace, mastering each one like a true kindness champion. Slow and steady wins the race (especially regarding kindness!).

5 **Sweet dreams are made of kindness.**
Before drifting to delightful dreamland, reflect on the acts of kindness you have done on that given day to ensure a peaceful, positive sleep.

6 **Feeling stormy?**
Kindness to the rescue! If you're worried or overwhelmed, grab this book and choose an exercise that will make you feel calm and relaxed. Kindness is like a magic shield that can deflect negativity.

7 **Make kindness your daily superpower.**
Promise yourself to do at least one act of kindness from each step daily. Because one is better than none. This builds positive habits that make kindness second nature, like getting dressed!

8 **Practice makes progress.**
Don't worry if you don't become **RICH IN KINDNESS** overnight. Keep practising, have fun, and remember that one is better than none and that every little effort counts! I promise that when you look back on your journey at the end of the book you will be delighted with all your progress.

REMEMBER, this book is just the beginning! Keep spreading kindness everywhere, making new friends, and inspiring others to join your quest. Together, we can create a brighter, kinder place, one act of kindness at a time.

BONUS TIP

Share your kindness journey with friends and family. Talk about what you're learning, and how good it is making you and others feel. Encourage them to join you and to celebrate each other's acts of kindness. Together, you can create a powerful ripple effect of positivity!

Now go forth, young adventurer, and let's connect on our first step to becoming **RICH IN KINDNESS** and get ready to spread your unique style of kindness! Remember, you have the power to make a difference.

If you are a child reading this, then skip to page 26. If you are an adult, then read on overleaf.

A TEACHER'S GUIDE

WELCOME, **TERRIFIC TEACHER!** You hold in your hands a powerful tool: **THE KINDNESS QUEST**, a treasure trove of activities and inspiration to guide your pupils on a journey to becoming champions of kindness. But how do you unlock its full potential in your classroom? Buckle up because we're diving into a world of kindness-filled learning!

SETTING THE STAGE FoR KINDNESS

★ Create a kindness corner:
Dedicate a space in your classroom for displaying kindness resources, such as inspirational quotes, books and materials for gratitude jars or compliment boards.

★ Establish ground rules:
Discuss and co-create classroom rules emphasising kindness, respect and empathy. Involve pupils in finding solutions for resolving conflicts peacefully.

★ Model kindness:
Embody kindness in your interactions with pupils, showing respect, offering encouragement and celebrating their efforts. Remember, actions speak louder than words!

EMBARKING oN THE KINDNESS QUEST

★ Choose your adventure:
Select activities from the book that align with your curriculum, learning objectives and pupils' interests. Adapt them to fit their key stage level and classroom dynamics.

★ Make it interactive:
Don't just read – do! Turn exercises into engaging activities like role-playing scenarios, group discussions or creative projects. Encourage pupil participation and collaboration.

★ Spark reflection:

After each activity, facilitate discussions about the experience. What challenges did pupils face? How did kindness feel to them? How can they apply this learning in their lives?

★ Celebrate success:

Recognise and celebrate acts of kindness, big and small. Use compliments, awards, or special privileges to reinforce positive behaviour.

SPREADING THE KINDNESS RIPPLE

★ Connect to the community:

Organise service projects or partnerships with local organisations, allowing pupils to implement their kindness in the real world.

★ Encourage kindness campaigns:

Empower pupils to design and lead initiatives to spread kindness throughout the school or community, such as organising a 'Random Acts of Kindness Day' or creating anti-bullying campaigns.

★ Embrace technology:

Utilise online platforms or apps to connect with other classrooms or schools engaged in kindness projects, fostering a global community of young changemakers.

REMEMBER

★ Be patient:

Cultivating kindness takes time and consistent effort. Celebrate progress, not perfection, and encourage pupils to learn from mistakes.

★ Have fun!

Kindness should be joyful and engaging. Infuse humour, creativity and playfulness into your activities to motivate pupils.

★ Lead by example:

Your enthusiasm and commitment to kindness will inspire your pupils. Be the kind, compassionate teacher you want them to become.

By using **THE KINDNESS QUEST** as a springboard, you can empower your pupils to become agents of positive change, building a classroom (and a world) overflowing with kindness, empathy and understanding. Remember, even the smallest acts of kindness can have a ripple effect, creating a brighter future for all. So, let's embark on this kindness adventure together and watch our pupils blossom into the kind, compassionate individuals we know they can be!

A PARENT'S / CARER'S GUIDE

WELCOME, AMAZING PARENT OR CARER! You're holding a key to unlock a beautiful treasure: **THE KINDNESS QUEST.** This book offers a treasure trove of activities and inspiration to guide your child on a joyful journey to become a beacon of kindness in the world. But how do you translate its magic into meaningful moments at home? **LET'S EXPLORE!**

BUILDING A FOUNDATION OF KINDNESS

★ Model kindness:
Your actions speak volumes. Be kind and compassionate in your interactions with your child, your family and strangers. Remember, you're their most significant role model.

★ Create a kind-focused home:
Establish ground rules emphasising kindness, respect and empathy. Encourage open communication and celebrate acts of kindness, big and small.

★ Embrace kindness conversations

Talk about kindness as a superpower! Read stories, discuss real-life examples and role-play scenarios to help your child understand the impact of their actions.

EMBARKING ON
THE KINDNESS QUEST

★ Make it a family adventure:

Choose activities from the book that resonate with your family dynamic. Adapt them to suit your child's age and interests. Turn them into shared moments of discovery and connection.

★ Spark creativity:

Don't just read, create! Transform exercises into games, art projects or even family challenges. Encourage your child to express their kindness in unique ways.

★ Reflection is key:

After each activity, have heart-to-heart conversations. Around the dinner table is a good place. Ask your child what they learned. How did it feel to be kind? How can they apply this new-found understanding in their daily life?

★ Celebrate every step:

Recognise and celebrate your child's kindness efforts, no matter how small. A warm hug, a sincere 'thank you' or a special privilege can reinforce positive behaviour.

SPREADING THE KINDNESS RIPPLE

★ Connect with community:
Look for opportunities to volunteer together or engage in acts of kindness within your community. Show your child that kindness extends beyond the family.

★ Empower kindness initiatives:
Encourage your child to brainstorm and lead their kindness projects. It could be baking cookies or cakes for neighbours or organising a toy drive. Let them experience the joy of making a difference.

★ Lead by example:
Show your child the power of technology for good. Support the online interactions that promote kindness and empathy and guide them from negativity.

REMEMBER

★ Be patient:
Cultivating kindness is a continuous journey. Celebrate progress, not perfection, and encourage your child to learn from their experiences.

★ Make it fun:
Kindness should be joyful and engaging. Infuse humour, creativity and playfulness into your activities to motivate your child.

★ Be their kindness champion:

Your unwavering support and guidance are invaluable. Be the kind, compassionate parent you want your child to become.

Using **THE KINDNESS QUEST** as a roadmap, you can nurture your child's inherent kindness and empower them to impact the world positively. Remember, even the smallest acts of kindness, when multiplied by your love and guidance, can create a ripple effect of compassion and change. So, let's embark on this beautiful journey together and raise kind-hearted kids who make the world brighter!

INTRODUCTION

'NO ACT OF KINDNESS,
NO MATTER HOW SMALL,
IS EVER WASTED.'

— Aesop

Ever wish you could have the coolest toys, fanciest clothes and biggest house on the street? **ME TOO!** I thought those things would make me super happy when I was young. But guess what? The feeling never lasted. Growing up in a single-parent household, I desperately dreamed of having lots of money and being popular.

Get rich quick ideas like winning the lottery or having lots of things may give you the illusion of being happy, but trust me when I say they can go as easily as they come.

But hey, I'm John Magee, the **KINDNESS COACH** and now the UK's Kindness Ambassador for Schools! And I'm here to tell you there's a different kind of richness that lasts way longer than any fancy gadget or cash: the riches of kindness.

You see, even though I didn't have mountains of toys and stuff, I always loved sharing what I did have with others. And guess what? Sharing kindness made me feel happier than any toy ever could.

Imagine life as a giant, epic adventure. The more kindness you share, the more awesome adventures you unlock – such as making new friends, helping others feel good, and spreading smiles everywhere!

REMEMBER that warm fuzzy feeling you get when you help someone? Or maybe you've seen someone else be super kind – how did it make you feel? Pretty great, right?

The super-wise Thích Nhất Hạnh once said,

> 'THERE IS No WAY
> To HAPPINESS,
> HAPPINESS
> IS THE WAY.'

This quote demonstrates that happiness is not a destination, it's a journey. It's about learning how to create your own happiness every single day as part of your daily adventures.

Imagine going on an incredible kindness adventure with awesome **KIND KIDS** like you, just like I did when I was young (and still do today!). We'll discover the secrets to becoming **RICH IN KINDNESS**, just like thousands of other **KIND KIDS**.

SO, ARE YOU READY FOR MORE...

★ ...friends who'll stick by you through your ups and downs?

★ ...gigantic grins and belly laughs?

★ ...confidence to shine like a champion?

★ ...adventures that make every day feel like a treasure hunt?

If you answered 'Yes' to any (or all!) of those, then read on and prepare to embark on this life-changing **KINDNESS QUEST**. We have six steps to unlock your inner **KINDNESS CHAMPION** and it all starts right now. With the star of this book... **YOU!**

SIX STEPS TO KINDNESS

STEP
1

KINDNESS TO YOURSELF

> 'TALK TO YOURSELF
> LIKE YOU WOULD
> TO SOMEONE YOU LOVE.'
>
> — Brené Brown

This chapter is all about cool ways to be kind to yourself. I want you to imagine that you have a big **KINDNESS JAR** ready to fill with gold coins. Each coin represents an act of kindness you do for yourself, and when you fill it up, it not only makes you feel great, but also fills you to the brim with confidence and currency to be kind to others too.

WOULD YOU LIKE TO LEARN NEW WAYS TO MAKE YOURSELF FEEL FANTASTIC?

Before you do this… Quick question! Do you ever feel upset? Worried or sad? We all do; I know I do sometimes, and it is perfectly normal to sometimes have uncomfortable feelings. But I have found a way to connect with my inner kindness champion and make myself feel better. This is the key to us embarking on this journey together and becoming **RICH IN KINDNESS**. Would you like to see how you can, too?

LET THE ADVENTURE BEGIN!

Imagine you're on a **KINDNESS QUEST**, not for some ancient treasure, but for something more valuable – **YOUR HAPPINESS!** This chapter is your secret map, packed with ideas to help you unlock the incredible power of being kind to yourself and learn a new way of finding the real treasure to becoming **RICH IN KINDNESS**.

WHY IS SELF-KINDNESS SUCH A SUPERPOWER?

As I said earlier, think of self-kindness as filling up a **KINDNESS JAR** with your gold coins. Every time you do something kind for yourself, that jar fills up with more gold coins. And guess what a full jar of gold coins means?

★ A confidence boost:

When you're kind to yourself, you whisper to your inner voice kind words like… 'I am amazing!'. And that's a great affirmation. Saying kind words to yourself, known as affirmations, will make you feel strong inside your mind and body and ready to tackle anything, like taking that test or making new friends.

★ Stress busters:

Feeling overwhelmed? It's perfectly normal to feel that way sometimes; even as a **KINDNESS COACH**, I have moments when I do too. But I make a daily effort to practise self-kindness by starting my day and being kind to myself. I see it like my magic shield against stress and uncomfortable feelings. Taking care of yourself teaches you to relax and recharge, like a world champion taking a positive power nap.

★ Happiness magnet:

When you're kind to yourself, you start to see the good things in life everywhere, like sunshine reflecting off puddles or the silly smile on your best friend's face. It's like wearing magical happiness glasses!

★ Kindness is contagious:

The most remarkable thing about self-kindness is its contagiousness! When you're kind to yourself, you naturally want to be kind to others, spreading happiness like dandelion seeds on a windy day, or as I say, **'SCATTERING SEEDS WITH GOOD DEEDS'**.

Now that you have learned some of the cool things practising self-kindness can do for you, are you ready to explore more ways to unlock how to become a champion of inner kindness, fill your jar with happiness, and start the journey to becoming **RICH IN KINDNESS?** Grab your trusty map (this chapter) and let's continue this incredible adventure together!

REMEMBER, every act of self kindness, big or small, takes you one step closer to your happiest, most confident self. So dive into the ideas in this chapter, take action, experiment, and find what makes your happiness jar overflow with treasure. The world needs your unique self, starting with the star of this book: **YOU!**

> 'YOU YOURSELF,
> AS MUCH AS ANYBODY
> IN THE ENTIRE UNIVERSE,
> DESERVE YOUR LOVE
> AND AFFECTION.'
>
> — Dalai Lama

SELF-KINDNESS IDEAS

Encourage yourself to be your own **KINDNESS COACH.**
Imagine a small, encouraging voice inside your head
reminding you of your strengths and offering kind words
when needed. The power of self-compassion can make a
big difference!

★ Positive affirmations:

Practise saying positive affirmations like '**I AM KIND**',
'**I AM BRAVE**', '**I AM CAPABLE**' and '**I AM CALM AND
PEACEFUL**' every morning, throughout your day and
before bed. Affirmations like these have been proven to
help boost your self-esteem and confidence:

'**I DEEPLY AND COMPLETELY
LOVE AND ACCEPT MYSELF.**'

'**I AM ALWAYS DOING MY
BEST UNTIL I FIND A BETTER
WAY OF DOING THINGS.**'

'**TODAY I LOOK AT ALL THE GOOD THINGS IN MY LIFE
AND I AM THANKFUL FOR THEM ALL.**'

'**I AM LOOKING FORWARD TO WHAT IS AHEAD.**'

★ Gratitude jar:

Each day, get a small piece of paper and write down something you are grateful/thankful for – big or small – and put it in a jar. Reading through the jar on tough days when your feelings or emotions may get the better of you (which, as I said, is perfectly normal), your gratitude jar can be a sweet reminder of the good things in life.

★ Calming corner:

Create a cosy space with comfy pillows, calming music and quiet activities like colouring, reading or deep breathing exercises. This can be a safe space to de-stress and recharge your good self.

★ Fill your cup first:

You can't share your kindness if you're running on empty! Keep practising the ideas in this chapter, from your gratitude jar to your calming corner. Make self-kindness a daily habit, like brushing your teeth, getting dressed and bathing.

★ Be your own kindness champion:

Don't wait for someone else to tell you you're amazing. Be your own biggest kindness cheerleader! Write down your fantastic qualities in a kindness journal and celebrate your achievements, big and small. In fact, I want you to go to the nearest mirror, look in it and say to yourself ten times: **'I AM PROUD OF YOU'**. Keep saying it and looking at yourself in the mirror. I wonder what other kind words you could say to yourself when you look at your beautiful face in the mirror?

CREATIVE KINDNESS

★ Kindness journal:

Write down or draw acts of kindness you can do for yourself or others. This can be a fun way to track progress and celebrate your good deeds. You don't need to buy a fancy journal if you don't want to; you can get a simple notebook and write down your thoughts. I love doing this daily as it helps support my mental health and wellbeing, and I feel great after writing my thoughts down and then reflecting on them.

★ Self-care day:

Plan a day dedicated to pampering! Take a bubble bath, watch a favourite movie (funny movies are my favourite…), bake cookies, or do anything that makes you feel good.

★ Positive visualisation:

Close your eyes and imagine yourself in a happy, peaceful place – perhaps a park, a beach, a familiar room – wherever you feel calm and relaxed. This can help reduce stress and anxiety.

★ Dancing:

Movement is medicine, so put on a song that you love and dance around freely to the music! Dancing is a great way to express your feelings and is proven to release endorphins (happy hormones) so not only will you get some exercise, you'll also get a boost of inner happiness. You could even create your own dance routine.

★ Creative writing:

Write a poem about kindness, or a story with a message of kindness, and share it with someone you love and respect.

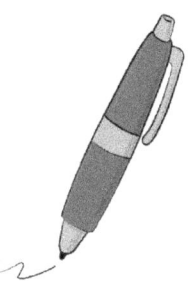

★ Drawing:

Draw a picture and colour it in and share with a friend who you consider to be kind.

PLAYFUL KINDNESS ACTIVITIES

★ Compliment kindness chain:

Start a chain of compliments by saying something nice about yourself. Like saying this affirmation to yourself and then sharing it with others: '**I AM ALWAYS DOING MY BEST UNTIL I FIND A BETTER WAY OF DOING THINGS**'. Then, take turns with friends or family members to compliment each other. This can spread positivity and build self-worth.

★ Treasure hunt:

Ask friends and family to write one positive thing about you on a sticky note and hide these around your room and in books, to be found as a nice surprise and a boost of motivation and encouragement when you're not expecting it. If you ask your terrific teacher at school for some sticky notes, I'm sure they will be very kind and give you some.

★ Kindness challenge:

Set a weekly or monthly goal for acts of self-kindness, like taking time for a quiet walk, saying no to something you don't want to do, trying a new healthy food you have not eaten yet, or aiming to drink two litres of water a day. Celebrate your achievements, no matter how small.

★ Puddle jumping:

Who doesn't love jumping in puddles when it's raining? Embrace your inner toddler, grab your wellies and jump in the biggest puddles you can find!

★ Rainy day jar:

Once you've found the same positive sticky notes (see above) put them in a jar, ready to open when you're having a rough day.

★ Snow angels/ kicking leaves:

Depending on the weather, if it has been snowing then go and create snow angels and take photos to share with friends and family, or run through big piles of leaves in the autumn, creating colourful waterfalls of leaves!

INTERESTING FACTS

THE SCIENCE OF
SELF-KINDNESS

Did you know that being kind to yourself is actually really good for you? When we're kind to ourselves, it makes our brains feel happy and connected, just like when we're with a good friend. Amazingly, taking care of our feelings can help us feel less worried and sad. It's like having a special tool to help us feel better! And guess what? People who are kind to themselves are better at bouncing back when things are tough. It's like having a superpower inside that helps us feel strong and brave.

HISTORICAL KINDNESS

People have been talking about being kind to yourself for a really long time. Ancient thinkers and wise people from different parts of the world understood how important it is to treat yourself with care. Even old traditions that teach us about being connected to nature and each other say that looking after yourself is part of looking after everyone. Today, we have special ways to help us be kind to ourselves, like thinking calmly about our feelings and sending ourselves good thoughts (affirmations). It's clear that taking care of our hearts and minds is something people have always known is important.

BoNUS TIP

Being kind to yourself is a journey, not a race to finish. It's OK if it takes time and there are ups and downs along the way. Remember, looking after yourself isn't selfish; it's like filling up your own jar so you can share kindness with others. When you're good to yourself, it shows others how to be kind to themselves too.

THE WORDS WE SAY TO OURSELVES ARE INCREDIBLY POWERFUL.

By telling ourselves kind and encouraging things, we can feel better about who we are and what we can do. When tough feelings show up, it helps to be gentle with ourselves instead of being mean. Saying something like, **'I'M FEELING FRUSTRATED, BUT THAT'S OK'** can make things easier. Plus, writing down things we're grateful for can help us see the good in life and feel happier.

FUN FACTS

Did you know that being kind to yourself is like giving yourself a big, warm hug? It feels good, right? And guess what? When you're kind to yourself, your brain releases happy chemicals that make you feel good. It's like having your own personal cheerleader inside your head! So go ahead, treat yourself with kindness — you deserve it.

> 'SELF-COMPASSION IS SIMPLY GIVING THE SAME KINDNESS TO OURSELVES THAT WE WOULD GIVE TO OTHERS.'
>
> — Christopher Germer

YOUR SELF-KINDNESS JAR RUNNETH OVER!

CONGRATULATIONS, ADVENTURER! You've journeyed through this chapter, unlocked your inner self-kindness superpower, and filled your happiness jar to the brim! It's time to take your new-found power and spread kindness across the land.

Remember, adventurer, the power of self-kindness is always within you. Use it wisely, spread it generously and watch your world become a happier, kinder place. Even the smallest acts of self-kindness ripple outward. Now go forth and conquer your next quest of becoming **RICH IN KINDNESS:** cool ways you can share your kindness at home.

I want you to write in this area
a minimum of three things you will
do to be kind to yourself.

SELF-KINDNESS IDEAS

I choose to...

CREATIVE KINDNESS

I choose to...

PLAYFUL KINDNESS ACTIVITIES

I choose to...

_____

_____

_____

_____

_____

_____

_____

What I enjoyed about this chapter was...

_____

_____

_____

_____

_____

_____

_____

_____

_____

KINDNESS AT HOME

'A HOME IS NOT A BUILDING, BUT A FEELING. IT'S WHERE KINDNESS RESIDES, LOVE IS EXPRESSED, AND HAPPINESS IS FOUND.'

— Unknown

I hope you enjoyed the last chapter, **FELLOW ADVENTURER**, learning how to be kind to the star of this book: yourself. What acts of kindness did you do to make your kindness cup overflow? Did you write them down in your to-do list? Good!

In this chapter, we continue on our kindness quest to become **RICH IN KINDNESS** and look at ways we can be kind at home. Being kind at home is super important. We can sometimes take all the kindness we receive at home for granted. I certainly did as a kid. Showing your gratitude at home is a great way to show kindness.

I want you to imagine your home as a beautiful garden where everyone's a friendly gardener. Kindness is like sunshine and water for that garden. When we're kind, it's like giving the flowers a warm sunbeam or a gentle sprinkle of rain.

Why is being kind at home so important?

As I said in the last chapter, think of it as filling up your happiness cup. Every time you do something kind, that cup gets fuller.

Being helpful is like picking up weeds.

Maybe your brother or sister spilt something, or your parent needs an extra hand carrying shopping. By helping, you clear the weeds of small tasks and make the garden grow strong.

Saying 'please' and 'thank you' is like planting colourful seeds.

These magic words blossom into beautiful flowers of appreciation that make everyone smile.

Sharing is like spreading pollen.

We all have unique talents and things we love, and sharing them is like spreading tiny pollen grains that make the garden colourful and fragrant for everyone.

Saying sorry is like planting a sunflower after a storm.

Mistakes happen, in the same way that storms can sometimes bend flowers. But saying sorry is like planting a bright sunflower that reminds everyone the sun will shine again.

Giving hugs and compliments is like watering flowers.

Everyone needs a little encouragement to grow tall and strong. A hug or a kind word is like a refreshing drink that makes the flowers perk up and bloom.

REMEMBER, even the smallest acts of kindness, like a tiny seed or a gentle breeze, can make a big difference in our home garden. So, let's keep spreading kindness and grow a garden of happiness together!

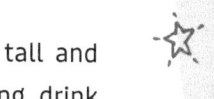

> 'KINDNESS IS THE GLUE
> THAT HOLDS
> RELATIONSHIPS
> TOGETHER.'
>
> — Unknown

KINDNESS AT HOME

★ The secret smile mission:
Secretly leave smiley face drawings or positive messages around the house for others to find, spreading unexpected joy.

★ Hidden helpers:
Complete small acts of kindness like putting away dishes or watering plants unseen, leaving a trail of helpfulness without expecting praise.

★ Chore buddies:
Partner up with siblings or parents to tackle chores together. Make it a fun team effort and celebrate completing tasks!

★ Helping hands:

Offer to help with daily tasks like setting the table, clearing dishes or taking out the rubbish. This small gesture can make a big difference.

★ Random acts of kindness:

Leave little notes of appreciation around the house, make someone's favourite breakfast in bed, or help fold laundry without being asked. These spontaneous acts show you care.

★ Thank you time:

Make saying 'thank you' a regular habit. Acknowledge what your family members do for you, big or small, and express gratitude.

★ Compliment corner:

Start a compliment board or jar where everyone can write nice things about each other. This can boost self-esteem and create a positive atmosphere in the household.

★ Love notes:

Leave secret love notes for family members hidden in their pockets or bags, or under pillows. These sweet messages can brighten anyone's day.

CREATIVE KINDNESS CHALLENGES

★ Chore charades:

Turn household chores into a guessing game where you can act out tasks for fellow siblings or parents to complete, adding fun to sharing responsibilities.

★ Build a kindness fort:

Gather blankets and pillows to construct a cosy fort, then make it a designated **KINDNESS ZONE** where family members can share kind words and gestures.

★ Sock rescue adventure:

Make rescuing lost socks from behind furniture a team effort, turning a mundane chore into a heroic quest. PS: don't forget the washing machine and dryer!

★ Random acts of creativity:

Leave silly drawings or funny poems hidden for family members to discover, or even create mini musical performances on the spot, sprinkling laughter and unexpected joy throughout the day.

KINDNESS CHAIN REACTIONS

★ The good deed domino effect:

Challenge yourself to do one kind act, then tell someone about it, inspiring them to follow suit and create a chain reaction of kindness.

★ Gratitude graffiti:

Use paper and colourful markers to write thank-you messages or compliments on sticky notes and leave them on doors, mirrors or furniture, spreading appreciation throughout the house.

★ Treat box:

Decorate a box and fill it with treats (ones your family likes – such as sweets, chocolate, fruit, stickers, etc). Encourage everyone to write down kind acts they've witnessed or done throughout the day. Draw a slip at random each evening and celebrate the chosen act of kindness as a family. The kindness champion of the day gets to pick a treat from the box!

EMPATHY AND CONSIDERATION

★ Listening ears:
Listen when family members talk and show interest in their day. This simple act makes them feel valued and understood.

★ Kind words:
Choose your words carefully and avoid saying anything hurtful or unkind. Remember, words have superpowers!

★ Helping in times of need:
Offer support and comfort to family members who are feeling down or going through a tough time. A hug, a listening ear or a small gift can make a big difference.

INTERESTING FACTS

THE SCIENCE OF KINDNESS:

'NO ONE HAS EVER
BECOME POOR BY GIVING.'

— Anne Frank

Being kind isn't just nice, it's actually really good for you! When we do something kind, our bodies release a special happy feeling that helps us feel connected and loved. Amazingly, being kind can even help us stay healthy and live longer. The best part is that kindness is like magic — it spreads! When you see someone being kind, it makes you want to be kind too. Let's work together to make our world a happier place, one kind act at a time.

HISTORICAL KINDNESS

Did you know that being kind has been cool for a really long time? People have been celebrating kindness for many years. There's even a special day every year, 13 November, just for doing kind things, called **WORLD KINDNESS DAY!** Wise people from all over the world have said amazing things about kindness. There have been champions of kindness throughout history, like Gandhi, who showed us how much one kind person can change the world.

FUN FACTS

Get ready for some fun facts about being kind. Did you know that giving someone a big hug is like wrapping them in a warm blanket? It's true! And guess what else?

Smiling is like magic! It's the easiest way to make someone feel happy, even if you don't say a word. Plus, doing something small and kind, like holding a door open, can make someone's whole day brighter. So let's spread smiles and warmth wherever we go.

BONUS TIP

Being kind doesn't always mean doing big, fancy things. Even small acts like saying 'please' and 'thank you', helping with chores, or cleaning up your mess can make a huge difference. Let's turn our homes into kindness gardens. Imagine planting seeds of kindness every day. Let's have fun with it and watch our garden of happiness grow.

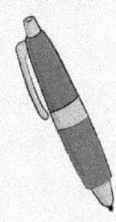

I want you to write in this area a minimum of three things you will do to spread more kindness around your home.

KINDNESS AT HOME

I choose to...

CREATIVE KINDNESS CHALLENGES

I choose to...

STEP
2

KINDNESS CHAIN REACTIONS

I choose to...

EMPATHY AND CONSIDERATION

I choose to...

What I enjoyed about this chapter was...

KINDNESS AT SCHOOL

'TREAT OTHERS THE WAY YOU WANT TO BE TREATED.'

— The Golden Rule

How did you get on in your last quest of being kind at home? Your riches are increasing and you undoubtedly scattered many seeds with your good deeds. Your heart, already glowing with the warmth of kindness, is ready to embark on a new quest through the wondrous halls of learning!

Let's continue our adventure together; I want you to imagine stepping through a magical portal at school - it transports you to a land of endless learning and adventure, where everyone is a fellow explorer on a shared quest for knowledge. Kindness is the secret map that guides our way, helping us navigate through challenges and celebrate victories together.

WHY IS BEING HELPFUL
AT SCHOOL IMPORTANT?

★ **Being helpful is like lending a compass:**
Maybe a friend gets lost in a maths maze, or their backpack gets weighed down with heavy rocks (aka difficult homework). Offer your compass of help, point them in the right direction, and lighten their load with a shared understanding.

★ Sharing ideas is like building a magnificent bridge:
We all have different views of things. Imagine these ideas are like colourful bricks. When we share them, we build bridges of understanding that connect us across rivers of doubt and help us reach new heights of knowledge.

★ Saying 'well done' is like lighting a bonfire:
Sometimes, the path ahead seems dark and scary. A simple 'well done' is like a crackling bonfire, casting warm light and encouragement, reminding everyone that we can conquer any challenge together.

★ Cheering each other on is like playing a
  drum of success:

When a friend does well in a test or stumbles through a presentation but keeps doing their best, give them a resounding drumbeat of successful support. Your cheers will fuel their courage and remind them they're not alone on this adventure. Remember the affirmation I shared earlier: **'EVERYONE IS ALWAYS DOING THEIR BEST UNTIL THEY FIND A BETTER WAY OF DOING THINGS.'**

★ Making someone laugh is like planting smiling sunshine seeds:

Laughter is like sunshine – it melts away clouds of negativity and makes the whole journey brighter. Plant sunshine seeds with a funny joke, a silly game or a goofy grin, and watch the entire land blossom cheerfully… (Example: 'In Maths, why is six afraid of seven? Because seven eight nine!')

REMEMBER, even the smallest acts of kindness, like whispering words of encouragement or sharing a giggle, can light the path for our fellow explorers. So, grab your **KINDNESS COMPASS,** build bridges of understanding, and light bonfires of support – let's make this school adventure one we'll never forget!

'PEOPLE WILL FORGET WHAT YOU SAID. PEOPLE WILL FORGET WHAT YOU DID. BUT PEOPLE WILL NEVER FORGET HOW YOU MADE THEM FEEL.'

— Maya Angelou

Here are some super-duper ideas for how to be kind in school.

SPREADING FRIENDLINESS IN SCHOOL

★ Greeting buddies:

Start your day by greeting classmates and teachers with a smile and a friendly hello each day. Ask them **'DID YOU DO ANYTHING NICE LAST NIGHT, YESTERDAY OR AT THE WEEKEND?'**. And listen to them speak: don't interrupt them, just let them express themselves. This simple act can brighten someone's day and make them feel welcome.

★ Inclusive play:

Invite new kids or other pupils you don't play with regularly to join games or activities during break or lunch. Show genuine interest in getting to know others and building friendships.

★ Kindness club:

Let your terrific teacher know you want to start a **KINDNESS CLUB** with friends where you share examples of how you can be kind inside school. For example, running a 'compliments day'. This can boost self-esteem, make you and others feel good, and spread positivity. 'You are doing a fantastic job on this journey!' (That was a compliment right there for you. How did that compliment make you feel?)

ACTS OF HELPFULNESS

★ Helping hands:
Help classmates struggling with tasks, carrying books or opening doors. Small gestures of support can make a big difference.

★ Buddy system:
Volunteer to be a buddy for a younger pupil, helping them to navigate the school, answering their questions, or simply being a friendly face.

★ Random acts of kindness:
Leave encouraging notes on classmates' desks, offer to share snacks, or hold the door open for someone. These spontaneous acts can brighten someone's day. Let your teacher know how grateful you are for them helping you get a good education.

EMPATHY AND UNDERSTANDING

★ Kind words:

Remember, words have superpowers! Choose your words carefully and avoid saying anything hurtful or unkind. Practise using inclusive language and respecting differences. Give this one a go. Say to a teacher, family member, friend or someone who works at your school **'YOU LOOK WELL TODAY'**. Notice how your kind words can brighten their day.

★ Listening ears:

Listen to classmates when they share their feelings or experiences. Show empathy and understanding, even if you don't always agree. It's perfectly normal to interrupt or want to get your point across when someone is speaking, but do your best to listen. Remember the phrase **'TWO EARS, ONE MOUTH'**. What needs to be done the most? Two ears (listening).

★ Standing up for others:

If you witness bullying or unkind behaviour, support the targeted person. You can report the incident to a teacher or offer friendship and support. There is no need for it to become physical. **REMEMBER THE GOLDEN RULE: TREAT OTHERS HOW YOU WOULD LIKE TO BE TREATED.**

PROMOTING INCLUSIVITY (BELONGING)

★ **Celebrating diversity (differences):**

Organise or participate in events celebrating cultural diversity at school, such as international days or cultural shows. This can help your understanding of different backgrounds. Remember kindness doesn't discriminate, and neither must you or anyone.

★ **Learning about others:**

Encourage your friends to learn about different cultures, religions and abilities. This can help break down stereotypes and build bridges of understanding. For example, all my family are Irish, and I am very proud of my heritage. Could you find out three interesting facts about Irish people? Or do the same for another country someone you know has links to?

★ **Welcoming newcomers:**

Make a special effort to welcome new pupils to the school and help them feel included. Introduce them to others, help them navigate the school, and show them your school spirit.

REMEMBER

★ Lead by example:
Other children learn by watching you. They will copy your kindness, which creates a kind and compassionate school environment.

★ Positive reinforcement:
Acknowledge and praise other pupils when you see them do an act of kindness at school. This reinforces positive behaviour and encourages them to continue being kind.

★ Open communication:
Talk to your friends about the importance of kindness and why it matters. Listen to their experiences at school and offer guidance if needed.

INTERESTING FACTS

SPREADING FRIENDLINESS
IS LIKE SPREADING SUNSHINE!

Just seeing someone smile can make you smile too, because our brains are wired to copy each other's happiness. Imagine how happy someone would feel if you greeted them in their own language. It's like giving them a special, friendly hug. And did you know that high-fiving someone can actually make you trust them more? It's true! So let's fill the world with smiles, kind words and high-fives!

HISTORICAL KINDNESS

WHILE THE CONCEPT OF KINDNESS
HAS EXISTED FOR CENTURIES,
TEACHING IT IN SCHOOLS IS A
RELATIVELY RECENT DEVELOPMENT.

Ancient philosophers and religious texts often emphasised compassion and empathy, but structured kindness programmes didn't emerge until quite recently. Early initiatives focused on character education and developing good citizenship, laying the groundwork for the comprehensive kindness curriculum seen in schools today.

FUN FACTS

KIDS ARE NATURAL-BORN KINDNESS EXPERTS!

They share toys, offer help, and celebrate each other's successes with pure joy. Sharing a smile, a kind word, or even a snack can make a huge difference in someone's day. It's like spreading sunshine throughout the school! Plus, when kids are kind to each other, it creates a magical atmosphere where everyone feels happy and safe.

'IF SPEAKING KINDLY TO PLANTS HELPS THEM GROW, IMAGINE WHAT SPEAKING KINDLY TO HUMANS CAN DO!'

— Tara Mackey

BONUS TIP

Imagine your school as a garden - you can help it grow into a kind and friendly place by being helpful and caring. By doing small acts of kindness, you can create a happier and more welcoming school for everyone - a place where kindness flourishes! Now, let's commit to some ways to unlock your **KINDNESS COMPASS** and continue your adventure!

STEP 3

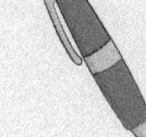

I want you to write in this area a minimum of three things you will do to spread more kindness around your school.

SPREADING FRIENDLINESS IN SCHOOL

I choose to...

ACTS OF HELPFULNESS

I choose to...

EMPATHY AND UNDERSTANDING

I choose to...

PROMOTING INCLUSIVITY

I choose to...

What I enjoyed about this chapter was...

KINDNESS TO YOUR FRIENDS

'A TRUE FRIEND IS ONE
WHO OVERLOOKS YOUR
MISTAKES AND ADMIRES
YOUR ACHIEVEMENTS.'

— Darnell Lamont Walker

How did you get on in your last quest to be kind at school? Your riches are increasing, and you are undoubtedly becoming richer in kindness.

Let's continue our adventure together as we look at cool ways to be kind to our friends and fill your jar with more kindness coins as we continue our quest to become **RICH IN KINDNESS**.

I want you to see your friends as your fellow treasure hunters on this amazing journey of life. Be kind, share your discoveries, and help each other uncover hidden gems (like shared jokes, secret talents, and supportive words) along the way. Kindness is the magical bridge that connects hearts and minds and turns your classroom or playground into a rainbow-coloured land.

WHY IS BEING KIND TO YOUR FRIENDS IMPORTANT?

Each kind word or helping hand becomes a colourful brick, building a bridge of understanding and friendship so everyone can reach the happy sunshine together. Sometimes, your friends may get a little cloudy on rainy days. Be a sunshine sprinkler! Sprinkle them with a smile, a silly joke, or a listening ear. Your kindness will chase away the rain and brighten their whole day.

SPREADING KINDNESS
CAN BE A SECRET MISSION!

Join the **SECRET SMILE SQUAD** and leave hidden smiles around the classroom/playground for your friends to find. A funny note, a surprise drawing, or even a friendly wave can spark a chain reaction of happiness. Think of your friends as fellow helping heroes facing the challenges of daily life. Be a caring, kind friend! Offer a helping hand with homework, share school equipment, or stand up for them when needed. **REMEMBER, TEAMWORK MAKES THE DREAM WORK** (and it spreads kindness like wildfire!).

'A FRIEND IS

SOMEONE WHO

KNOWS YOU AND

LOVES YOU ANYWAY.'

— Maya Angelou

Here are more cool ways to be kind to your besties... who will undoubtedly become your **BFFs** (**BEST FRIENDS FOREVER**)!

SPREADING KINDNESS AMoNG FRIENDS

★ **Be a good listener:**

Give your friends attention when they talk; show empathy and avoid interrupting.

★ **Offer support:**

If they're feeling down, offer them a hug, a word of encouragement, or simply be there to listen.

★ **Celebrate friends' successes:**

Be their biggest cheerleader! Be genuinely happy for their achievements and accomplishments and let them know.

★ **Offer help without being asked:**

If you notice any of your friends struggling with something, offer a helping hand. I suggest helping them carry their belongings, offering to study together, or running errands.

★ **Show appreciation:**

Don't take your friendship for granted. Tell them how much you value them and appreciate their presence.

SOME MORE KINDNESS ACTIVITIES

★ Include everyone:
Make sure that everyone feels welcome and involved in games, activities and conversations. Don't leave anyone out.

★ Share and take turns:
Be fair and generous when sharing snacks, playing games or choosing activities. Learn to compromise and consider everyone's preferences and feelings.

★ Offer encouragement:
Cheer on your friends during competitions, games or even when trying something new. Positive support can boost their confidence and make them feel good.

★ Be a good sport:
Win or lose, be gracious and respectful. Congratulate the winner and accept defeat with a smile. Remember, friendship is more important than the outcome.

★ Stand up for friends:

If you see your friends being treated unfairly, speak up and defend them. There is no need for physical force; be their voice when they need it and report it to an adult.

CREATIVE KINDNESS

★ Leave surprise notes:

Hide uplifting messages or funny drawings in their locker, backpack, lunchbox or desk. These little surprises can brighten their day.

★ Do something unprompted for friends:

Make them their favourite snack, offer to walk their dog, or help them with a project without asking.

★ Plan a fun outing:

Organise a picnic, film night or game night for the two of you. Spending quality time together strengthens your bond. (Turn off your phones and focus on the time together.)

★ Create a friendship memory box:

Collect photos, ticket stubs, souvenirs, or any mementoes that remind you of fun times you've shared.

★ Pay attention to friends' hobbies and passions:

Show them you care about their interests. Surprise them with a themed card or handmade gift, or simply have a conversation about what they love.

REMEMBER,
FELLOW ADVENTURER:

SMALL GESTURES MATTER.

Who will you be kind to today? A fellow adventurer, a new face, or someone who seems alone? Remember that every act of kindness, big or small, lights up the path for others. So, go forth and be the hero of someone's day!

Congratulations on finishing today's quest of kindness. But remember, the adventure never ends. Keep your **KINDNESS COMPASS** aimed true, your smile sword sharpened, and your helping hand ready because tomorrow brings a new journey with your fellow adventurers to share. Onward to more kindness magic!

'FRIENDSHIP IS
A PRECIOUS THING.
DON'T GO AROUND
THROWING IT AWAY.'

— Shirley Temple

INTERESTING FACTS

FRIENDSHIP IS AMAZING!

Did you know that laughing together actually makes your brains work together, as if by magic? And guess what? Having good friends can help you stay healthy and even get smarter! It's true! Giving someone a high-five can make you trust them more, and hanging out with happy people can make you smile too. By being kind and supportive to your friends, you can create a world where everyone feels happy and connected. Isn't that cool?

There are over 200 languages worldwide, but there's one universal way to say 'friend': a smile!

HISTORICAL KINDNESS

LONG BEFORE SOCIAL MEDIA AND SMARTPHONES,
PEOPLE FOUND CREATIVE WAYS TO
SHOW KINDNESS TO THEIR FRIENDS.

Ancient Greek philosophers emphasised the importance of loyalty and friendship, while Roman friendships were often marked by shared experiences and mutual support. In medieval times, knights swore oaths of loyalty to their companions, demonstrating the enduring value of friendship through history.

FUN FACTS

KIDS ARE MASTERS OF KINDNESS.

Sharing and caring, offering a listening ear, or simply being there for a friend in need are acts of friendship magic. Friends build forts of trust, laugh together until their sides ache and create memories that last a lifetime. It's like spreading sprinkles of happiness everywhere they go!

BONUS TIP

Kids are champions of kindness! They share their treasures like true champions, offer support with unwavering courage, and listen with champion ears. Their laughter is a powerful weapon against boredom, and their friendship is a force for good.

I want you to write in this area a minimum of three things you will do to spread more kindness to your friends.

SPREADING KINDNESS AMONG FRIENDS

I choose to...

SOME MORE KINDNESS ACTIVITIES

I choose to...

CREATIVE KINDNESS

I choose to...

What I enjoyed about this chapter was...

STEP 5

KINDNESS TO YOUR COMMUNITY

'ALONE,
WE CAN DO SO LITTLE;
TOGETHER,
WE CAN DO SO MUCH.'

— Helen Keller.

AHOY, **FELLOW ADVENTURER!** Remember how we filled our jar with kindness coins with our BFFs... Now, it's time to grab our backpacks and embark on a new quest: spreading our kindness and treasure in our community. But wait, this isn't a solo mission. We're in this together, a whole crew of **KINDNESS CHAMPIONS.**

So, tune up your smile-o-meters, polish your good-deed goggles, and get ready to make smart choices in your community, so it sparkles brighter than a dragon's hoard of gold. Because your community is the land of adventure and kindness is the secret map that leads us to laughter, support and the ultimate treasure – a community filled with happy faces!

So, are you ready to set sail on this kindness ocean with your awesome, kind crewmates? Then, let's dive in and discover the coolest ways to be kind to our fellow community members and make sure everyone's **KINDNESS JAR** overflows!

WHY IT IS IMPORTANT TO BE KIND TO YOUR COMMUNITY

Human beings were designed for community. Everybody needs to feel that they belong and are connected to something. However, in an age of AI, social media and online activities, staying 'connected' is ironically harder than ever! A lot of people find it difficult to make new friends or find opportunities to connect with those around them. By spreading acts of kindness in your community, you may well draw in those who feel left out and make a positive difference to someone's day. We can all achieve much more together than we can alone.

'EVERYONE YOU MEET
IS FIGHTING
A BATTLE YOU KNOW
NOTHING ABOUT.
BE KIND. ALWAYS.'

– Anonymous

Here are some cool kindness activities you can apply in your community. You will need an adult to help you with most of these.

BUILDING ON YOUR KINDNESS SKILLS

★ Homegrown helpers:

Remember filling your home garden with kindness seeds? Now, let's plant those seeds in the community! Offer to help at a local park clean-up or volunteer at an animal shelter to walk furry friends.

★ Lead the way:

Hold the door open, next time you notice someone behind you.

★ Handmade cards:

Make some handmade cards that sparkle with positive messages and send them to a local hospital or nursing home for the staff and patients.

★ Sharing the sunshine:

Just like sprinkling sunshine at school, sprinkle smiles in your town! Leave cheerful chalk messages on the pavement, organise a community singalong or bake some cookies for local firefighters, care workers or NHS staff.

★ Kindness compass guides:

Remember navigating with your **KINDNESS COMPASS** at school? Now, be a guide for someone else! Help someone new to your local community find their way, teach younger kids a new skill, or offer to be a reading buddy at the library.

★ Visit a local nursing home:

Spend time reading to someone, playing music, or simply having conversations. Bringing joy and brightening the day for others can be an incredibly rewarding experience.

SHARING TREASURE WITH OTHERS

★ Share that smile:
Challenge yourself to smile at everyone you see on your walk to school.

★ Waste-busting wizards:
Organise a neighbourhood clean-up day, plant trees or seeds in a local park, or create upcycled crafts from recycled materials. (We will talk about this in our next kindness quest.)

★ Helping hands for tiny feet:
Being small doesn't mean your kindness can't be big! Help younger children cross the street or offer to carry groceries for elderly neighbours.

★ Organise donations:

Gather unused toys, clothes or books and donate them to local shelters, religious centres or charities. Spreading generosity helps those in need and teaches valuable lessons about giving back.

★ Organise cultural exchange events:

Host potlucks where people bring dishes from their cultures, share stories about their traditions and learn simple phrases in different languages. These foster understanding and appreciation for diversity.

★ Learn about local history and cultures:

Visit museums, historical sites or cultural centres to learn about the history and traditions of your community. This will help you to understand the unique stories and contributions of different people.

CREATIVE KINDNESS ADVENTURES

★ Kindness compliments:

Try to compliment three people you see that day. It could be about something they've made, or something they're wearing, or something you think they're good at. Compliments are a great way to show people that you notice them and appreciate them.

★ Kindness artwork:

Remember spreading smiles with silly jokes at school? Paint your community with positivity! Create pavement chalk art with uplifting messages, organise a community mural painting project, or leave funny riddles hidden around town for others to find. (Make sure to get permission first.)

★ Random acts of kindness fairies:

Surprise your community with tiny bursts of kindness! Leave encouraging notes hidden on car windscreens, plant surprise flower seeds in public spaces, or anonymously pay for someone's coffee at a local cafe.

★ Community talent show:

Showcase your kindness and superpowers! Organise a talent show where everyone performs acts of kindness – singing songs, helping people in need, or creating art to brighten someone's day.

★ Plant a community garden:

Work with neighbours to plant and tend a garden. This helps with environmental awareness, provides fresh produce for those who need it and fosters a sense of community spirit.

REMEMBER: Every act of kindness, big or small, ripples through the community. Encourage your fellow adventurers to choose a quest that speaks to them and watch their kindness light shine bright.

INTERESTING FACTS

KINDNESS IS LIKE MAGIC DUST
THAT TRANSFORMS COMMUNITIES.

A simple smile, a helping hand or a thoughtful gesture can brighten someone's day and create a ripple effect of positivity. By choosing kindness, we not only uplift others but also enrich our own lives. Let's be the champions of our communities needs by spreading kindness far and wide.

HISTORICAL FACTS

OUR WORLD IS A VIBRANT TAPESTRY
WOVEN FROM COUNTLESS THREADS
OF DIFFERENT CULTURES AND BACKGROUNDS.

Let's celebrate this beautiful diversity by embracing our differences and treating everyone with kindness and respect. By working together and including everyone, we can create a world where everyone feels valued and belongs.

FUN FACTS

COMMUNITIES ARE BLOOMING WITH KINDNESS!

People are lending a helping hand to neighbours, volunteering their time at local shelters and supporting small businesses. From organising community clean-ups to donating to food banks, these acts of generosity are creating a ripple effect of positivity, bringing people together and strengthening the bonds of community.

> 'THERE IS No POWER FOR CHANGE GREATER THAN A COMMUNITY DISCOVERING WHAT IT CARES ABOUT.'
>
> — Margaret J. Wheatley

BoNUS TIP

Encourage your fellow adventurers to write down their kindness adventures. Take pictures, write stories or draw pictures to share your experiences with others and inspire more acts of kindness. Together, you can make our community a kinder, happier place, one adventure at a time!

I want you to write in this area a minimum of three things you will do to spread more kindness around your community.

BUILDING ON YOUR KINDNESS SKILLS

I choose to...

SHARING TREASURE WITH OTHERS

I choose to...

CREATIVE KINDNESS ADVENTURES

I choose to...

What I enjoyed about this chapter was...

KINDNESS TO THE PLANET

AHOY, FELLOW ADVENTURERS! Remember how we filled our cups with kindness to the brim and spread sunshine among our communities? It's time to expand our quest and embark on a new adventure! Buckle up your green thumbs and unleash your inner eco-heroes because this time, we're setting sail for the most amazing land of all: our beautiful Earth! Also known as 'the Planet'.

'TO LEAVE THE WORLD BETTER THAN YOU FOUND IT, SOMETIMES YOU HAVE TO PICK UP OTHER PEOPLE'S TRASH.'

— Bill Nye

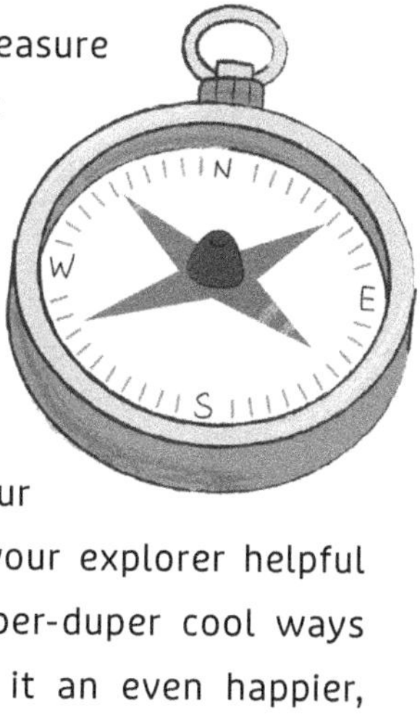

Think of our planet as a giant treasure chest overflowing with wonders - sparkling oceans, towering trees, playful animals, and even the air we breathe! But just like any treasure, it needs our care and kindness to keep it shining bright. So, grab your

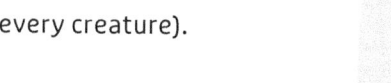

KINDNESS COMPASSES, put on your explorer helpful hat, and get ready to discover super-duper cool ways to be kind to our planet, making it an even happier, healthier place for everyone (and every creature).

'A SINGLE ACT OF KINDNESS
THROWS OUT ROOTS
IN ALL DIRECTIONS, AND
THE ROOTS SPRING UP
AND MAKE NEW TREES.'

— Amelia Earhart

WHY IT IS IMPORTANT
TO BE KIND TO THE PLANET

Scientists tell us that changes are happening to our world because of something called climate change. Part of our responsibility as caretakers of this world is to look after it, and there are lots of things we can do. It can feel a little overwhelming when we think of the big picture. So it's best to start small and think: **'WHAT CAN I DO TODAY? HOW CAN I BE KIND TO THE PLANET IN MY HOME OR MY GARDEN?'** Millions of kids just like you are already making a difference, and you can too. Every small step, from recycling to protecting wildlife, helps to create a healthier planet for everyone. Let's work together to build a brighter future for everyone!

Are you ready to:

★ **plant seeds of kindness that blossom into a greener, cleaner world?**

★ **become a nature detective, solving puzzles to protect amazing animals?**

★ **be Earth's recycling superstars, transforming trash into dazzling treasures?**

★ **join a global kindness chain, connecting with others who share your love for our planet?**

Then, let's dive in. This chapter is your secret map, packed with exciting ideas to unleash your inner Earth-loving hero and become **RICH IN KINDNESS,** one eco-friendly adventure at a time. Remember, every act of kindness, big or small, makes a difference; so grab your boots, get ready to explore, and let's show our planet some profound love.

Here are some cool ways to be kind to our planet:

GROW YOUR GREEN THUMBS

★ Seed-sowing superstars:
Turn your garden, balcony or windowsill into a mini forest! Plant flowers that attract pollinators like bees and butterflies, or grow your fruits and veggies – healthy for you and the planet.

★ Compost crew:

Don't throw away food scraps! Start a compost bin and turn it into nutrient-rich soil for your plants, reducing waste and feeding the Earth.

★ Tree huggers unite:

Organise growing a plant or a tree with your family or friends. Plants and trees give us oxygen, clean the air, and provide homes for animals – a triple win for kindness!

BECOME NATURE DETECTIVES

★ Wildlife whisperers:
Learn about local birds, insects, and other creatures. Build a bird feeder, create a butterfly garden or leave out water bowls for thirsty animals. Every living thing deserves our kindness. (Hedgehogs are my favourite.)

★ Beachcombers for good:
Organize a beach clean-up and collect plastic waste. Imagine the joy of sea turtles and ocean creatures swimming in cleaner waters!

★ Eco-explorers:
Discover the wonders of nature near you. Visit parks, forests or even your backyard, observing plants, animals, and the amazing ecosystems they create.

RECYCLING ROCKSTARS

★ Rubbish transformation challenge:
Turn old boxes, jars or clothes into something new and amazing! Craft birdhouses, planters or even costumes – unleash your creativity and reduce waste.

★ Recycling rangers:
Learn about different recycling symbols and teach your family and friends. Organise a neighbourhood recycling competition – the greenest bin wins!

★ Upcycle extravaganza:

Give old toys, clothes or books a new life. Donate them, organise a swap party, or get creative and turn them into something completely different.

JOIN THE GLOBAL KINDNESS CHAIN

★ Spread the word:

Share your eco-adventures with others. Write letters to local newspapers, create posters or even start a blog to inspire others to be kind to the planet.

★ Connect with eco-buddies:

Find friends who share your passion for the environment. Create a school eco-group, participate in environmental groups, or even start your own club at school.

★ Support awesome eco-heroes:

Research organisations working to protect the planet and find ways to support their efforts. You could raise money, volunteer or even write letters of appreciation.

REMEMBER, FELLOW ADVENTURER: Every act of kindness, big or small, makes a difference for our planet. So, get creative, have fun, and keep exploring ways to be the best Earth hero you can be. Together, we can make our planet a happier, healthier place for everyone.

INTERESTING FACTS

OUR PLANET IS AN AMAZING
PLACE FILLED WITH INCREDIBLE
LIVING THINGS.

Imagine a single tree breathing in as much pollution as a car creates every year. Planting one is like having a world champion boxer fighting pollution. Bees are tiny but mighty, visiting hundreds of flowers in one trip to help them grow. Every time we help a bee or plant a tree, we're writing a small part of Earth's amazing story. Let's be champions of kindness for our planet!

HISTORICAL KINDNESS

Throughout history, humans have developed a deep connection to the natural world, often reflected in spiritual and cultural practices. Indigenous cultures revered the Earth as a mother, inspiring stewardship. Ancient civilisations like the Mayans and Incas developed intricate agricultural systems that worked in harmony with nature. While these early practices focused on survival, they laid the foundation for modern environmental consciousness and inspire our efforts to protect our planet today.

FUN FACTS

RECYCLING IS SUPER POWERFUL — JUST ONE ALUMINIUM CAN CAN LIGHT UP YOUR TV FOR HOURS!

Recycling aluminium is a highly efficient and environmentally friendly process. By recycling just one can, you can save enough energy to power a TV for hours, reduce landfill waste, conserve natural resources, and decrease greenhouse gas emissions. Additionally, recycling aluminium supports domestic industries and creates jobs. It's a simple yet powerful act that contributes to a sustainable future.

Composting food scraps turns leftovers into garden magic.

Planting trees has many benefits.

Kids are planet-saving champions. They can turn recycling into a fun game, plant seeds with champion strength, and protect animals with incredible care. Their imaginations transform everyday actions into exciting adventures, like being water-saving detectives or energy-saving wizards. They are proof that even small hands can make a big difference for our planet.

BONUS TIP

Track your positive progress and document your eco-adventures. Take pictures, write stories, or draw pictures to share your experiences with others and inspire more acts of kindness.

Let's continue to fill our jars with kindness and spread it across the planet, one adventure at a time. Everyone, no matter how young or small, has the power to make a difference for our planet. So, let's start our kindness adventure today and everyday make the world a greener, kinder place together!

'WE ARE THE FIRST GENERATION TO FEEL THE IMPACT OF CLIMATE CHANGE AND THE LAST GENERATION THAT CAN DO SOMETHING ABOUT IT.'

— Barack Obama

I want you to write in this area
a minimum of three things you will do
to show more kindness to the planet.

GROW YOUR GREEN THUMBS

I choose to...

BECOME NATURE DETECTIVES

I choose to...

RECYCLING ROCKSTARS

I choose to...

JOIN THE GLOBAL KINDNESS CHAIN

I choose to...

What I enjoyed about this chapter was...

A SPARKLING CONCLUSION

YOU'VE DONE IT! YOU'VE COMPLETED THE KINDNESS QUEST. I want you to take a moment to think about everything you have achieved through reading this book and all the people you have been kind to. It may have taken you out of your comfort zone, but you tried it anyway, and I'm so proud of you!

I'm willing to bet that you have made a positive difference in your school, at home, with your friends, in your community and to the planet. The ripples that you created won't stop when you turn the last page in this book. Kindness continues and kindness is contagious.

REMEMBER, one act of kindness is better than none, dear adventurer; your quest for kindness doesn't end here! The book may end, but your journey to become **RICH IN KINDNESS** continues.

CARRY THE LESSONS OF THIS BOOK LIKE PRECIOUS TREASURES IN YOUR HEART.

★ Kindness is a superpower:

It has the magic to light up someone's day, build bridges of understanding, and fill your jar with happiness.

★ Every act counts:

No matter how small, your kind deeds ripple outwards, creating a wave of positivity that touches more lives than you know.

★ Start with yourself:

Be your kindness champion, treat yourself with love and respect, and watch your inner light shine even brighter.

★ Spread the joy:

Share your kindness like contagious laughter, inspiring others to join your quest and make the world kinder.

Remember, becoming **RICH IN KINDNESS** is an ongoing adventure. There will be stumbles and challenges, but always remember the power you hold within. Let your smile be your sunshine, your words be your encouragement, and your actions be your testament to the incredible kindness inside you.

So go forth, young adventurer, and continue to paint the world with kindness! Remember, the world needs you and your unique brand of goodness to make it a brighter, more compassionate place.

A FEW LAST THOUGHTS

★ **How could you create or keep a KINDNESS JOURNAL to track your progress and acts of kindness, big and small?**

★ **Imagine what would happen if you were to create a KINDNESS CLUB with friends or classmates to spread kindness at school or in your community.**

★ **I'd like to know what inspiring stories of real-life kindness heroes you could share with others to motivate them to become RICH IN KINDNESS.**

May you have everything you need on your life journey and may it be filled with kindness, happiness and joy!

Thank you for your kindness.

YOUR KINDNESS COACH

JOHN MAGEE

THE KINDNESS MATTERS COMMUNITY

YOUR KINDNESS QUEST CONTINUES ON YOUTUBE!

Are you ready to supercharge your kindness journey and connect with a community of fellow adventurers? Dive into the world of **KINDNESS MATTERS TV** on YouTube. KMTV is aimed at schools around the UK and globally, helping them to cultivate kindness inside and outside the classroom.

Search for **KINDNESS MATTERS TV** on YouTube, find **THE KINDNESS QUEST** section, and you'll unlock a treasure trove of resources to take your practice to the next level. Watch me share inspiring videos, learn new things, and discover ways to teach kindness to an adult family member or friend (remember, sharing is caring!).

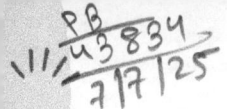

WHY JOIN THE KINDNESS MATTERS TV COMMUNITY?

★ **Become part of a tribe:**
Connect with other **KIND KIDS** who value belonging to a tribe of like-minded people. Support your mental health and wellbeing, and find calm amidst the everyday rushing around.

★ **Discover new tools:**
Expand your kindness toolkit with engaging video content that teaches how to create more kindness in the world and more.

★ **Level up your kindness:**
Learn from fellow **KIND KIDS** experts and fellow kindness champions, gaining valuable insights into becoming **RICH IN KINDNESS** and creating lasting positive change.

★ **Remember, you're not alone in this quest.**
KINDNESS MATTERS TV is your virtual hub for support, inspiration and endless possibilities to grow your inner **KINDNESS SUPERHERO.**

So, what are you waiting for? Grab your virtual backpack, hop on YouTube, and join the adventure. **REMEMBER**, the more kindness we share, the brighter the world becomes. Now, let's pass it on together!

Comment on one of the **KINDNESS MATTERS TV** videos, sharing your favourite part that you read and actioned from my book or your personal experience. Let's spread kindness and love!